Karma in Action

"Short. Simple. And profoundly valuable."
—*Steve Pipe,* business author and UK Entrepreneur of the Year

"Kindness and service are powerful human forces that make a real bottom-line difference in business. Kudos to Joanne for *Karma in Action* and making kindness a practical business skill for everyone."
—*Ron Kaufman, New York Times* best-selling author, founder of UP! Your Service

"A poignant and timely reminder that the corporate world as a whole has gone through a cathartic change in the last two decades. Leadership is about empowering those whom you serve. What legacy will you leave behind? How will your teams remember you in ten years' time? A highly recommended book by a true modern-day renaissance thinker."
—*Hema Prakash,* Head of APAC Mindbody, former board member Monster.com

"Simple, clear, focused, clean, opening and revealing. Love it, Joanne and Booth. It is actually coming at the right karmic moment for me to ReThink! Thanks for sharing your wisdom."
—*Kevin Cottam,* author of *The Nomadic Mindset: Never Settle . . . For Too Long*

"'Whatever you want to experience abundantly in your life, first give it to others,' says Joanne Flinn, who generously gives us *Karma In Action.* Who knew 'gardening' could offer such kind business growth? But when you follow these five steps, not only will you plant your Karma, but you'll reap so much more—because Karma works."
—*Jac Phillips,* Senior Director, VISA

Karma in Action

How to use **karma** and **kindness**
to grow your business

Bonus: Your Karma Journal

By Joanne Flinn

the Business Growth Lady

Illustrations by Booth Aster

Author: Joanne Flinn
Illustrations: Booth Aster
Editor in chief: Anna Flinn
Copy editor: Louisa Bennion
Layout: Karl Hunt

Appreciation credits: Geshe Michael Roach, Lama Christie McNally, and Michael Gordon for *Karmic Management*. Geshe Michael Roach for *The Diamond Cutter* and *The Karma of Love* and the Diamond Wisdom team for all the wonderful workshops.

ISBN: 978-0-9943233-3-0

A CIP catalogue record is available for this book from the National Library of Australia.

2nd edition 2020

Thank you to all the grand masters
who've helped me grow

Table of Contents

Foreword

You know how it is.

There are times when you need not so much a friend, but you'd really love to *hang out with one* for a while.

You'd love to sit, share, sip a tea or sparkling water—or maybe something stronger.

And you'd love to reveal things that you've been thinking and wondering about. Like, "Why am I feeling this way about that?" "How on earth could I handle this issue in a way that makes everyone feel better about it?" "How do I suggest to Jane that what she's doing here doesn't feel right?"

Those kind of intimate things you'd only share with special friends—friends who bring no judgment, friends who'd listen more than tell while you find your own deep truth.

This wonderful little book is that friend.

So, treasure it—even hug it. The words and the beautiful illustrations will make you want to do that.

And then look at yourself in the light of the book.

The result will be wonderful.

And then, just as this book actually gives in other ways too (see page 15), you'll want to give even more of yourself AND you'll want to share it with friends who will love the book too.

That way, more giving gets done all around.

And karma and kindness become ever more a part of your world . . . and ours too.

Love,

Paul Dunn

Chairman of B1G1

Karma in Action

If you've ever lived the logical world of business success and secretly wanted a kinder way of being successful, this is the book for you.

I did. I went out looking for other ways, tried them, and watched other people do these same things. I have distilled that wisdom into this short book, dedicated to you.

Among the many benefits of Karma in Action, you will:

- Get lots done while feeling calmer than normal
- Do nice things for yourself and for others—as an official part of being successful
- Find yourself more creative and insightful

Sound good? It is. It's deliberately using the wisdom and traditions of karma in a modern, organized style. It's the best of both worlds.

It's the Golden Rule in Action.

You'll learn how to start your day well, finish your day well, and do good as you go along. It's all deliberately, mindfully simple.

Where did this come from? Well, first a little about me. I put in my years in the hard corporate world and wanted to find a way to work that was based on kindness and consideration, yet still got things done.

I was introduced to the principles that became this book by a friend, Lynna, who pointed me in the direction of Geshe Michael Roach and, through him, the teachings of the Dalai Lama. The practices in this book are based on ancient wisdom. The approach and structure are thoroughly modern.

Over the years I've used the simple practices described here for writing other books, for creating TEDx Talks, for raising capital, for business transformation, and even for making art.

I've come to appreciate karma as seeds that I can plant and then cultivate and watch ripen.

I like that I can be responsible for what I see happening around me and change it. I love that this approach adds to the kindness I experience in my life. I love that it's helped me become more aligned with my spirit. Amidst the busy noise of the modern world, it's added to my ease and relaxation.

The first edition of this book came out in 2015 as *Karma and Kindness*, a simple, practical tool that helped me each day. It's my secret sauce! Others tried it and shared it forward.

This edition is the next iteration of those time-tested ideas, designed to help you get things done, be successful, and enjoy your life.

Hugs and love,
Joanne & Booth

Yeah! You are here! Have you got something you wish to get done?

There is something wonderfully satisfying when you deliberately put karma to good use.

Pick a project, something you'd enjoy and appreciate having completed. It may be a particular goal for your business, for example, to increase sales or get that digital project done. Or it may be something you've hoped to achieve in life, like getting fit or feeling more relaxed.

This simple, effective book is designed to help you work with karma as a tangible tool. This book will help you move from karma being an idea to karma being a way of doing things.

Fundamentally, it's a deliberate way of working with your mind so that it becomes a tool that helps you create the world you'd really prefer to have around you.

This practice is built on two concepts:

- Our mind creates everything[1]
- We can plant mental seeds to grow what we want around us

---

1   I was thinking of calling this book *Quantum and Karma* because the mind's ability to influence the physical is very much in alignment with the principles of quantum physics.

When you are successful with your project, here's a hint: share these concepts of karmic management with others, and spread the seeds of kindness to make a difference. The wise say sharing good things helps many people.

This book is organized into three parts.

(1) Getting It Started
(2) Getting It Done
(3) Your Karma Journal

To help you put this into practice, as a much-appreciated reader of this book, go to:

www.karmainaction.works/KIA

for a karmic reward and an extra getting-started program.

PART 1

Getting Started

What is it? *It* is whatever project you've decided to do. Now, as we said before, this may be a personal goal or it may be something that your boss has just assigned to you, like, "Grow the business by 100,000 thingos in six months." Pick a project that's really important or that just puts a smile on your face. Whatever it might be, you've chosen your practice run for trying out Karma in Action.

Ready to take the next step? You'll like this part. Take this book to a spot that is your quiet space and let's get into a new (but very old) and more successful way of doing things.

Use this workbook in your quiet thinking space.
A cup of tea is also nice!

CONGRATULATIONS
ON DOING
SOMETHING
NEW!

Your Karmic Project

What project would you really like to complete or see happen?

_____

_____

_____

_____

_____

_____

_____

_____

_____

_____

One job you would really like to get done in your life right now

_____

_____

_____

_____

_____

_____

_____

_____

_____

_____

You'd like to have this done by

_____ / _____ / _____
(day)   (month)   (year)

Yes, we are getting straight into it—practicing motion rather than thinking about what we could be doing.

Let's keep gently moving forward.

Exactly how will it look if you are really successful at this task?

Note: *Specifics! Let your imagination fill this page in. Color if you like, little sketches too. It's all good.*

STOP DOING THINGS
THAT DON'T WORK

"All failure comes from misunderstanding."
                              – The Wheel of Life, 500 BC

Let's explore for a moment. Why do things in a particular way that only works some of the time? This uncertainty can be really unsettling and draining. Try this out.

Write five things you have to get done this week

1. _____ _____

2. _____ _____

3. _____ _____

4. _____ _____

5. _____ _____

Next to each item, write down the odds that you complete it exactly as you want to this week.

Reflect on the pressure of these odds and reflect on what this uncertainty means. What effect does it have on your life?

Now change all the odds to 100%. How does this make you feel?

Notice the difference in your feelings between doing things with the odds being uncertain and doing things when you are sure of the results.

START DOING THINGS
THAT DO WORK

"When that happens, this happens."
—The Buddha, 500 BC

Karma is what's going on under the hood of life . . .
what is really making the wheels go round.
It's like the starter on a car.

Karma is what we do to others, coming back to us. Karma is a seed. It's small things which then come back to us as big things.

Write three of the most successful things that have ever happened in your life

1. _____

   _____

2. _____

   _____

3. _____

   _____

Looking back, whom did you help similarly good things to happen for, even in a much smaller way?

1. _____

_____

2. _____

_____

3. _____

_____

Notes: *In karmic thinking, what we do to or for others is like planting a seed in the garden of our mind. It takes root and grows. And we get it back, bigger than what we planted.*

Identify Your Karmic Business Partners

"The First Law of Karma:
Whatever you want from life,
You must do for someone else first."
—Jey Rinpoche (1357–1419),
teacher of the First Dalai Lama

Karma works. What goes around comes back to you. So, if you want success, give success to someone else. If you want time, give time. If you want money and abundance, give money and abundance. If you want respect, give respect.

"But wait," I can hear you saying, "I don't have enough of these things to be giving them away." In karmic terms, however, we've all got enough to give, and we've got to give to get. The good thing is, seeds are small. Give what you want to others in small, deliberate ways.

It's about making others more successful. Happier. Richer. Healthier. More capable.

Whatever you want to experience abundantly in your life . . . first give it to others. When you make them successful, you become successful, too.

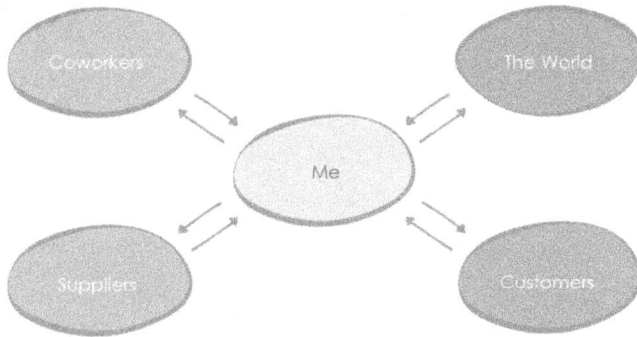

In business, think about these four groups of people. Coworkers, suppliers, and customers are usually pretty easy to identify. If you are starting out, find people who represent these groups for your future business.

How do you help the world, even when you feel small?

Doing good in small ways that ripple out big has never been easier, thanks to 21st-century interconnectedness. No matter what size your business, you can do good in the world through small micro-giving.

Take a look at www.B1G1.com, for example. B1G1 helps businesses aid people in need through micro-giving, which is one way of planting seeds.

B1G1 selects and vets NGOs across the world for you to choose from on their platform. To use me as an example of how this works in practice, each time my business Project Wings helps a client achieve an important goal, the money we receive for that work also helps someone else in the world. Each time I sell a book, I contribute using B1G1's platform so that a family in Africa can have access to clean water. When I check my weekly book sales, I'm thinking not only about the good I've hopefully done for my readers, but about how my book sales have contributed to the prosperity of faraway people I don't know and who don't know me. One drop at a time, I'm making a powerful difference.

If this idea resonates with you or inspires you, look at www.b1g1.com/connect. It's totally worthwhile. It's allowed my business to have its own Foundation and do good *now*, without waiting until we are huge.

If you'd like to join, you can use the code KIA or the link https://b1g1.com/connect/KIA. B1G1 will connect you to me with this code, so that all our giving and kindness is visible as a collective network of karmic change-makers in the world. We can make an amazing amount of karma together.

ACTION: Identify one specific individual for each type of Karmic Business Partner.

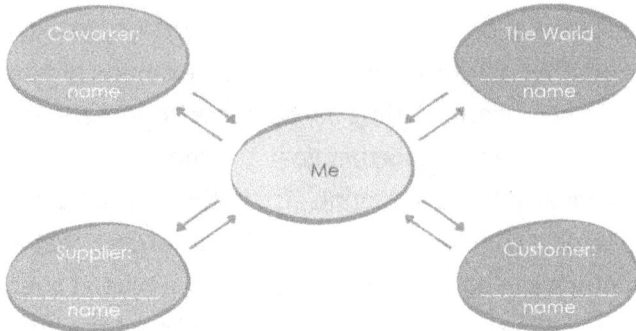

Now, what will their success look like?
Nothing big, perhaps, but be as specific as you can.

Adding fertilizer to the process.

What is the essence of what you want for yourself? Find a karmic partner who wants the same thing. This requires observing what is really important to the other person rather than imposing what *you* want for them.

If you can, find and help someone who is helping lots of people. By helping them, you create greater ripple effects.

While I'm on the topic of fertile soil, helping people who have helped you is super powerful. Parents are good as they gave us life. Teachers too.

Helping those in need is also karmically awesome for both them and you.

START FROM YOURSELF

"The line between me and you is artificial."
—Master Shantideva, 700 AD

In karmic terms, you have to make the first move if you want to see something arrive or change in your life. Unilaterally.

You have to start making your karmic business partners successful first.

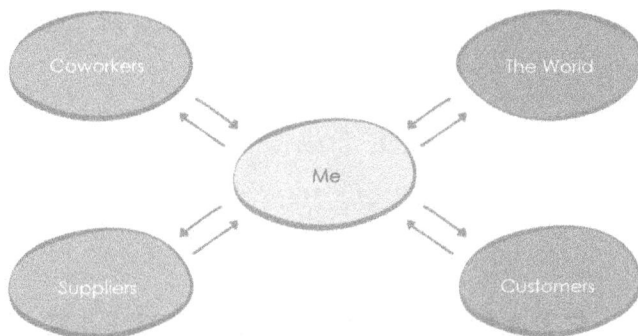

ACTION: Draw a circle around all the karmic business partners you've identified. Yes, this is the big *You*. In karma, helping others is helping yourself in the biggest sense.

Doing nothing means you get nothing back.

If you want something in your life (like success, health, wealth, and happiness) you must do something first. And when you do, you will get it back.

Now, let's talk business. What about competitors? Do you need to help them too? Yes, help them with the best intent of your heart, because . . . you guessed it—what goes around comes around.

When you act in true, big-picture collaboration, that pie, and everybody's piece of it, gets bigger and bigger.

Yes, this is the really, really big **You.**
Now draw a circle all the way around
the edge of the page!

Nine Actions for Karmic Fitness

So, starting with you . . . karma needs you to be healthy and have a clear mind. Karmic fitness means physical, mental, and emotional fitness first.

1. Do yoga—daily.

   Check out Lady Niguma yoga—it is lovely! Explore nearby yoga studios till you find a form and teaching style that fits you.

2. Meditate—daily.

   Look around, as meditation can take many forms. You can begin with a practice as simple as shutting your eyes, noticing your feet on the ground, and breathing in and out three times slowly. Prayer is a powerful form of meditation too.

3. Personal ethical code.

   Your code will be personal (obviously!) but it should cover, at a minimum:

   Respect for life + respect for others' things + respect for relationships + respect for words (speak the truth).

4. Keep learning.

   Notice what really is happening, particularly how when you change the way you look at things, what you say to people, and what you do to others, things change for you. Thoughts, words, and actions are all seeds.

5. Serve others.

   Doing things for others is fundamental; you've got to do for others what you want for yourself. Doing things they need, and without any expectations attached, is an act of service.

6. Eat skillfully.

   Eat fresh where possible. Watch the carbs and fats for better energy. For stronger eco-karma, consider the vegetarian option!

7. Rest, relax, and reduce clutter.

   Reduce mental chatter by being mindful about your exposure to the internet and news, and clear out your home of things you don't use often.

8. Commit constant, conscious small acts of kindness.

   Plant kindness seeds for yourself!

9. Reflect on your day and the good you've done.

   This is like watering and fertilizing your good karma.

Each of these actions plants seeds of self-care, calm, and kindness. You are doing quite a lot of good here while being good to yourself!

Look at each of these as helping you be a better gardener.

To help you put this into action, here are some practical steps to develop your skillfulness.

Skillful Noticing of Yourself: Practice mindful eating

Get started today. Are you putting things into your system that might slow it down or speed it up?

Fuel	Sugars	Carbs	Fats	Stimulants	Other
Meal					
Snack					
Meal					
Snack					
Meal					
Snack					

You've remarked that this is called skillful noticing. As you notice what works for your body, deliberately do a bit more of what works.

Karma is a bit-by-bit method. Little bits add up over time to become greater than their sum.

> **Note:** *Sugars and sugar substitutes!*
>
> *Carbs include bread, rice, and pasta ... all the processed stuff!*
>
> *Limit your fats, particularly the saturated or processed sorts.*
>
> *Stimulants include coffee, nicotine, black tea, and even green tea.*
>
> *"Others" includes drugs and alcohol, which alter mind and mood.*

Living into Your Ethics and Intention: Write up your personal ethical code

Here's a sample list to get your ethical juices flowing:

1. *Have faith in people's good intentions and seek to under-stand before I react or judge.*

2. *Look after the planet by carbon-balancing my travel.*

3. *Respect my body by eating nutritiously and getting enough sleep.*

4. *Be careful to say what I truly mean and feel, and to say it respectfully.*

5. *Respect relationships and hold them in a place of honor and delight.*

Note: *It's your code, so you're writing it just for you and it might not make sense to anyone else. It's lovely when other people understand your code, but it's not about whether they approve or not.*

Now, write out five principles that you wish to live by

1. _____

_____

2. _____

_____

_____

3. _____

_____

_____

4. _____

_____

_____

5. _____

_____

_____

Noticing your actions in a relaxed, appreciative way

Today as you go to bed, think of which of these you had the most success with. *Write it down in a single sentence.*

Personal **Ethics** In Action

And then enjoy an end-of-day meditation.

Peppermint Tea Meditation

This is the secret sauce: calm, relaxed appreciation of your day and the seeds you've planted with acts toward others.

Enjoy a cup of tea, relax back with your head in that position we used for daydreaming as kids, and simply recall what you've done intentionally for others today.

This is karmically watering the seeds you've planted.

Advanced Peppermint Tea Meditation. Two variations for you:

1. Think about the good things you've done on other days, too. There is no time limit on this meditation!

2. Meditate on all the wonderful people who helped put the many things in place that helped you today.

    For example: my cup of tea. I can meditate on the people who grew the peppermint, picked it, dried it, then packed and distributed it. The logistics guys who got it to me, the brand and company that markets it. Oh, and there are the pipe layers and the ones who make sure I have clean water in the tap!

STOP MAKING DECISIONS

"Not this. Not that either."
—Nagarjuna the Wise, 200 AD

Have you noticed that there are things that have a natural sense of flow and rightness and then there are things that require decisions? Decisions can bring a sense of stress with them. Decisions lead to the uncertainty of *will it work*? By contrast, when something's right, it feels clear and easy.

Let's explore what happens when we go into the pros and cons space, a classical tool for making decisions.

> **ACTIVITY:** The pros and cons list. This is the logical way to deal with decision-making.

Go back to your five tasks for the week from page 9.

For each task and for the way you plan to do it, what are three pros and three cons? Use the template for each task below.

Task 1:

Pros	Cons

What might go wrong? Are there cons for the pros and pros for the cons, if you get what I mean?

Now, how does it feel to make a decision about what to do?

☺ 😐 ☹   Circle the one that applies.

Task 2:

Pros	Cons

What might go wrong (those pros and cons to the pros and cons)?

Now, how does it feel to make a decision about what to do?

☺ ☺ ☹   Circle the one that applies.

Task 3:

Pros	Cons

What might go wrong (those pros and cons to the pros and cons)?

Now, how does it feel to make a decision about what to do?

☺ ☺ ☹   Circle the one that applies.

Task 4:

Pros	Cons

What might go wrong (those pros and cons to the pros and cons)?

Now, how does it feel to make a decision about what to do?

☺ ☺ ☹   Circle the one that applies.

Task 5:

Pros	Cons

What might go wrong (those pros and cons to the pros and cons)?

Now, how does it feel to make a decision about what to do?

☺ ☺ ☹   Circle the one that applies.

Instead of worrying about pros and cons, get clear on what you really want and get your seeds ready! Remember, karma in Action is about doing for others, in relaxed, happy confidence that it all comes back to you.

If you feel tension from the pressure to make a decision or if you feel yourself going into the pros and cons space, take a step back and work out what it is you really want. Maybe the decision you're getting so stressed out over is completely unnecessary. Then plant seeds by helping someone who also wants the same thing.

READY YOUR SEEDS

"The Fourth Law of Karma says no action is ever lost."
—Jey Rinpoche (1357–1419) teacher
of the First Dalai Lama

No action is ever lost. Now, before you panic about letting go of making so many decisions, or that you have too much to do, reflect. What are those Nine Actions for Karmic Fitness really about, and what do they do for you? What's really going on?

Maybe those Nine Actions are also to help you be more connected to the bigger picture and tune into your gut instincts, your intuition.

Hmmmm. Interesting.

Ah, do you get it? Let's step back to business. Remember your Karmic Business Partners? They represent the bigger you. By helping your Karmic Business Partners to succeed, you are helping the bigger *You* succeed. All these actions come back to you.

START DOING SMALL, THOUGHTFUL ACTS OF KINDNESS

The little things you do today will grow into the bigger things you see happening around you. Karma is a mirror of what we've done to others. Actually, it's a bit like an echo that comes back later—and louder. It's even more like planting seeds: some will fall on the ground and won't grow well, while other seeds you plant will grow into wonderfully big karmic trees.

ACTION: Every day before you start work, write down one specific action you can take to make each of your Karmic Business Partners more successful. Later, as you do the action, tick it off as *Done*.

Karmic Partner	Who	What	Done
Coworker			
Customer			
Supplier			
The World			

Note: *It does not need to be big. It probably shouldn't be. Just one thing you can honestly get done today that will contribute to* **their** *success.*

Make this a habit for the rest of your life.

This is all you need to do.

Note on the note: *This is easier than our mind wants to make it. Small good things add up.*

STOP WORRYING ABOUT PROBLEMS

"Your problems are your path."
—Geshe Potowa, Tibetan monk, 1027–1105 AD

So, you are doing good and seeing good come back to you, but stuff keeps happening! What's happening?

Problems are old seeds ripening.

Oh. Stuff that you did in the past. That stuff comes back, too.

Think of it as a bunch of weeds that already began growing and that need to be pulled out.

Or if you like flying, it's like you've got a bunch of other planes on the runway that need to be cleared before all the good new stuff can take off.

Earlier seeds in the queue to take off

So . . . what problem seeds from the past might sprout (or are bearing fruit already)?

Ask yourself, "What did I do to another that might have planted this seed?"

For example, you notice customers are often late for meetings. You feel your time is wasted and not respected. Ask yourself, "Where am I doing something like this to someone else, even in some small, tiny way?" It may be saying you were going to call your mother at a particular time and being a bit late, or simply being a bit late for meetings yourself.

Then, to weed the seed and clear the plane (and to mix our metaphors while we're at it!), what do you need to do now? Whatever it is you've been doing to others to plant that seed, stop doing it right away.

Geshe Michael Roche tells the story of the pen. To you, it's a tool for writing. If a dog comes into the room, he sees something he can chew. Both you and the dog are right. Now, when you and the dog leave the pen in a room alone, what does it become?

For you to see the pen, you need to have the seed of the pen in your mind. The pen-ness of it comes from you.

If you perceive it, you have the seed for it. Which means you can change how you perceive things, too.

Intent is at the heart

What's going on here, at a fundamental level? The intent in your heart is powerful. This small seed in your heart can grow into a mighty tree.

Karma and the Golden Rule

In the spirit of doing good to others, when bad comes back to you, the healthy karmic approach is to say, "I don't know what's happening in their heart." For example, some years back when I was running a business during the Global Financial Crisis, we had to change people's jobs. We had to let some people go. It was rough.

Those affected might have thought we were being political or mean or unkind. As for myself, I was focused on looking after the business and the people as well as I could. In some cases, it meant releasing people early so they could find a new job before it got worse.

A few months later, we made the business decision to shut down my division and I myself was let go. At one level, this can be viewed as my karmic seeds bearing fruit. And yet my colleagues did it with good recommendations, removing a restraint of trade clause in my contract and doing what they could to help me move forward. Karmic seeds at another level...

Rough seeds ripen. What we plant comes back to us.

At one level, this is super relaxing: there is no need to get angry or feel vengeful or frustrated. Let karma be in action.

Now, when you notice bad things happening to you, see it as seeds ripening. You can celebrate and say, "Yeah, the crop is in, and those seeds have run their course."

More proactively, you can clear out those seeds. Many of us have done things that, well, we regret. Instead of letting them grow into some huge tree, clear them out. See them as weeds.

You have four powers for weeding seeds. Use these to clear planes from the runway and weeds from your garden.

1. Remember it all comes from you (picture the pen).
2. Intelligent regret: yes, you did something whose results you don't like.
3. Promise yourself not to plant that same mistake of a seed again (make this promise to cover a specific period of time).
4. Do something positive to balance the karma. Plant a good seed!

ACTION: Clearing Problem Planes

Write down three actual or potential problems you see coming up that could prevent you and your team from successfully completing your project. Then think about what seeds you might unknowingly have planted to result in these problems.

For example, say your problem is that customers are paying late, thus creating cash-flow worries for your business. Are you doing something yourself that resembles this? Maybe you're paying your suppliers right on the last day of the billing period, or even a day or two late. Some companies do this as a matter of practice, but in karmic terms this could be the cause—the seed—for your problems with your own customers. What to do? Pay on time if you'd like to be paid on time. Pay early if early payment would make you happy!

Problem 1:_____

_____

_____

What do I do that is seeding this? _____

_____

_____

What I can do to change it: _____

_____

Problem 2: _____

_____

_____

What do I do that is seeding this? _____

_____

_____

What I can do to change it: _____

_____

_____

Problem 3: _____

_____

_____

What do I do that is seeding this? _____

_____

_____

What I can do to change it: _____

_____

_____

REINVEST THE KARMA

"Karma consumed dies."
—*Master Vasubandhu,*
Indian monk, 350 AD

Plant seeds ... cultivate ... harvest ... replant 10%!

Gratitude lets you celebrate the success of your project with each Karmic Business Partner.

> *The karma of celebrating this kind of success is*
> *itself the most powerful karmic seed of all!*

It's positive feedback in action!

Think about karma like a plant. It's grown into a nice big apple tree. If you just ate the apples and never planted any new trees, eventually your apple tree will die, and you'll be without apples. Good karmic practice is to take 10% of what you make and replant that. Farmers regularly hold 10% of what they've harvested and hold it for the next season.

This is really what we are doing, deliberately giving forward so we have what we want in the future.

In business terms, take 10% of your profit and invest it forward into helping your business partners. Here are some ideas:

- It's always wonderful to be thanked, to receive a gift, or to be invited to a celebration. There are ways of appropriately saying, "Thank you for being part of this."
- Find ways to thank suppliers, as they are key to your success. Maybe you introduce them to another client; maybe you give them a good performance bonus or take the time to craft a thoughtful recommendation that will help them stand out to prospective clients.
- Contribute to the world. There are endless ways to give forward (look into B1G1, as discussed on page 15, for example).

Start Celebrating

Give gratitude that extra energy by putting that 10% to good use for all your karmic partners.

Go back to page 16. What are simple things you can do to show your gratitude and appreciation for each Karmic Business Partner you identified there?

Build this into your project plan or business process.

And do it.

Stop Stressing

Being stressed is the opposite of being relaxed and enjoying life. However, some of us need the adrenaline fix that comes with stress to feel like we're accomplishing something. Do you see being busy as being successful?

It's not the same thing.

Busy ≠ Success

Great creativity needs a clear, relaxed mind. How can we get to that state?

ACTION: Skillfully Noticing Your Mind Clutter

Before you go to bed, record for today:

1. Exact number of minutes on your computer/devices: ____

2. Did you take a break every 30 minutes? ____

3. How much news did you read/listen to? ____

4. How much not-strictly-necessary time did you spend on the phone? ____

Your aim, over time, is to reduce things that create mind clutter (unncessary screen time, news, or gossipy chitchat) and increase the things that keep your mind clear, like taking breaks regularly, having good conversations, and doing meaningful work.

★ ★ ★

Wonderful! You've got all the pieces now. You know your project and your karmic partners, and you've learned about the nine actions that help you be in great shape as you plant your karma. You've also learned about some of the things that get in the way—the old stuff that still sprouts up like weeds. Now it's about actually doing those small actions.

And re-investing your karma!

It's time to get it done.

PART 2

Putting Karma and Kindness into Action

"How does this work at the day-to-day level?" I often get asked.

Here is an example of one way to put karma into action and get a faster start to using kindness and the power of karma in your business and life. This is how I went about setting up a project near to my heart, and one that I was certain would do good in the world.

Big Goal: Project Wings Pte Ltd: A thriving business that helps leaders who are making big positive changes in the world succeed faster.

What we do: we coach and train people how to get things done, and then we help them do those things. Think of this as a combination of leadership and mind-set coaching along with innovation and project and change management. Our clients range from solo entrepreneurs to IBM executives.

"We help you get your important projects done serenely and swiftly." (Do you get the wings bit? ☺)

To support this goal, I identified four elements:

1. Enjoyable fun work
2. Creating a healthy, sustainable world
3. Being valued—wealth and money
4. Being a great leader

I share how these break down into karmic actions on the next few pages.

Pick elements that are important to you. To continue the example over the next few pages is an expanded version of each element outlined above, in action.

The daily karma and kindness planner is helpful in making progress each day. You can find this tool in the next section and use it to set your goals, identify your karmic partners, and do a bit each day to create prosperity and success.

Enjoyable and Fun Work

To plant seeds for this: in identifying my karmic partners I specifically focused on my team and people in a supplier relationship to my company.

I looked for things that they enjoyed. For example, some of them liked to laugh and do things together. I deliberately made sure they could do this each day. Others wanted to celebrate little successes; one person loved a good glass of champagne! Another, a supplier, really appreciated being acknowledged for their attention to detail.

I'd focus on a different person or supplier each day. I'd deliberately notice something and plant a seed. I'd join in the laughter or make a joke. I'd notice the little success and do bubbles. Sometimes it was sparkling water; other times, yes—champagne ☺. I'd pay attention to what my suppliers did and say I'd noticed that little detail. I'd email their boss. At the end of a project, I'd write a great recommendation.

In the first week, the seeds were tiny and I couldn't see much change. During week two, there was more laughter around. By week four, I noticed I'd stopped being so serious and was enjoying what we were doing. I can say from my own experience that doing things from joy is much more fun than simply doing them out of discipline.

Creating a Healthy, Sustainable World

To plant seeds for this, we look at the impact of what we do. I mentioned earlier that one of my values is a living planet. As part of what my company does (and I do this for my personal life too), we track our key activities. This allows us to identify and offset each activity that creates an environmental impact. We also give forward using B1G1.

For example:

When we fly, we plant trees to offset the CO_2 emissions. We count our driving miles and offset these as well. We plant good seeds for the participants in our programs by contributing to education and clean water in needy parts of the world.

We are always working towards offsetting the energy we use and the food we consume.

When we buy products or services, we look for partners who are also balancing their footprint on the planet. Our goal is to have all our supplier partners fully sustainable by 2025, and we encourage our customers toward sustainability too.

At a personal level, I'm working towards offsetting my entire life by 2022. Each of us makes a difference, and I want mine to be a difference for the good.

At the global level, there is so much to be done for sustainability.

What we do supports this movement by helping create demand for services and products that will help solve the bigger problems and make our world one we want to live in 20 years from now.

On our small daily level, how does this come back as a karmic echo?

I'm amazed at things like how often we get great seats at restaurants, how we got upgraded into a better and more lovely space at the co-working office we use, and the gifts that arrive to help us be healthier.

Being Valued—Wealth and Money

To plant seeds for this, I differentiated three forms of wealth. The first was the freedom to choose when we work (time), the second was being appreciated (value), and the third was cash flow (money). Each form of wealth required different seeds and karmic partners to grow and flourish.

To plant and grow time freedom, I focused on our customers, deliberately making sure we helped them get things done when *they* needed them done. As trust is something that grows over time, we've seen our customers move from being very date-focused to being much clearer about their priorities, letting go of absolute deadlines to be much more flexible in balancing the inevitable changes that happen when dealing with complex moving parts in a project.

The result for us was much more choice on when we do things. For example, knowing that time was somewhat flexible, we could allow ourselves a mid-afternoon movie or a two-day retreat to recharge.

In terms of being valued and appreciated, I focused on the team and suppliers, using a similar process to the fun example on page 44. The difference was that I looked for things that they were doing well, and each day I'd make sure to express appreciation. Sometimes it was a compliment or an email saying I'd noticed, other times it was a surprise voucher for something they liked or an actual gift of a book, chocolate, gym time, or movie time. A LinkedIn recommendation and a written referral can be good too.

Over time, as these seeds blossomed, we got compliments in return. Clients referred us forward, and their appreciation took the form of opportunities that I never would have imagined.

To cultivate money and cash flow, I focused on being simple and clear about our service charges for customers and being meticulous with paying our suppliers as swiftly as possible. I realized that by waiting till the 30-day mark, I was holding onto flow and paying late. This was an ingrained habit, as I'd worked as an executive in a business that had a practice of paying late using 90- and 180-day credit terms.

It took some time for me to clear those seeds off my runway. But I did, and these days, clients put down deposits and pay ahead. They say they like keeping us in motion!

Being a Great Leader

To plant leadership seeds, I began with some reading and realized that this is a twofold goal, to be achieved both by trusting in my vision as a leader and by gaining the trust of my team.

To plant trust seeds, I focused on my customers and employees.

With my customers, I made a point of looking at each comment they made as coming from a space of good intentions. This involved some weeding of my old seeds. My business background had me viewing all feedback as negative, even when it was meant to be constructive. I realized I needed to be much more clear in my own heart, when giving feedback to my employees, to be sure that it came from a true intention to help us all be better.

I also learned that each day with my team I could simply plant seeds of being clear on my vision and goals, then trusting team members, in my heart, to get on with it. Over time, when we'd do check-ins, our conversations moved from that wary reporting-to-the-boss thing to respected humans contributing to a bigger outcome.

The same seeds led to similarly wonderful results with my clients and customers!

In practice: Find the essence of the various elements of your goals. While you can look to mine as an example, my story represents only one way of seeing a situation. Remember the pen story too!

Getting to the Essence:
More Examples

You've got to get to the essence of what things mean for you in order to work out what to give to others.

Remember to give to someone who wants the same thing as what you want!

Here are some examples. Note: the essence is personal. These general outlines are here to help you in the process.

Things you may want in your business and life	Essence
Revenue/income	Value. This can be valuing what you have, valuing what others have given you; valuing others.
Sustainability	Respect for environment and resources that support you and others; avoiding wastefulness.
Employee moral	Love for/appreciation of people and what they do and bring.
Being relaxed as the founder	Ease in decisions; ease in finding resources; competent, engaged team.
Being relaxed as an employee	Calm, competent team and boss. Be calm and give this to others; help your boss and colleagues get their work done when you have extra skills.
Getting referrals	Being trusted to do great work. Give trust by trusting others to do good work. Make sure your own comments come from a kind heart.

Things you may want in your business and life	Essence
Having great customers	Doing things you love for those you love; respect and enjoy.
	Help others match up with good partners.
Having more time	Feeling there is enough time.
	Respect time; help others get their work done so they have more time.
Having great business partners	Doing things you love with those you love; respect and enjoy.
	Help others match up with good partners.

Clearing Up Common Business Problems

Old stuff is like weeds that need to be pulled out or planes that need to be cleared off the runway. Celebrate successful weeding! See the four powers on page 39.

Things that may be happening	Essence and what you can do to balance
Not getting paid on time?	Are you paying people late?
	Deliberately pay people ahead of time.
Not getting paid what you're worth?	Are you being tight with money or devaluing others' work?
	Deliberately look at others and appreciate what others are creating. Look at where you can value people. Pay full price. Give a bonus. Give with a heart full of generosity.

Things that may be happening	Essence and what you can do to balance
Not getting enough customers?	Are you holding back from referring or recommending others? Deliberately recommend people, help other people to get customers, help them with marketing, help them refine their message.
Not having really lovely customers or a really lovely boss?	Where are you not appreciating and celebrating what others are doing for you? Deliberately notice what your team and suppliers are doing. Thank them. Appreciate the little places where they pay attention to detail.

Now at its heart, karma is a daily practice. Each day I'll do something small and seed-like for my karmic partners. I'd pay attention to the nine daily actions.

I use the Karma Journal to help me plan my day and track what I've actually done. The journal helps me to:

a) Stay relaxed and easy
b) Celebrate as I made progress

I've included an example of one of my days.

Then following the example, you'll find your Karma Journal. It's a bonus from us to help you get into flow and stay in karmic action.

If you'd like to jump right in, get support for your efforts, or even explore a deeper program on Karma In Action, please go to www.KarmaInAction.works/KIA where more resources await you.

Hugs,
Joanne & Booth

DAY & DATE: Monday, 28/10/2019

Plan Your Beneficial Actions for Today

Karmic Partner	Who	What	Done
Coworker	Cheri	Cheri appreciate the design she is developing	✓
Customer	Fred	Send a cheerful note to encourage their progress, + big! the new agreement	✓
Supplier	John	Pay invoice and send note so they know its done	✓
World	Planet	Offset the paper and energy we use today	✓

Creative space to riff, draw, and write notes:

Journal

Online support
? a fortnightly mentoring

Book to publisher

THEN launch party!

For the new year 'how to'

Checkin in a quarter how is it feeling?

DURING THE DAY: Do your beneficial actions! (tick them off as you go)

Skillful noticing: Eating

Are you putting good fuel or poor quality fuel into your system?

Fuel	Sugars	Carbs	Fats	Stimulants	Other
Meal	Fruit			Coffee	
Snack					
Meal		Rice	Minor		
Snack	Fruit				
Meal		Sweet potato	Cheese		Wine
Snack					

Skillful noticing of your mind in action (circle or check where appropriate)

Your words: Your actions:

(kind words) idle chatter   (thoughtful) disruptive   Watch out for talking over others, make sure they've finished

You took a break every 30 minutes ✔

BEFORE YOU GO TO BED: Skillfully notice

1. **Your intentions:** Beneficial actions done as planned? (Yes) No

2. **Your mind:** (minutes on)

On the computer / devices: **540**   News: reading or listen to: 10   Unnecessary time on the phone: 0

3. **Yourself in action:**

Ethics in action: Personal act of kindness:

In alignment   Calling T re her father

Now fall asleep thinking of the good things you've done today!

Your Karma Journal

Begin with Your Karma Project

Now, put karma in action each day with the kindness daily planner and karma journal. Things usually happen faster if you do good each day!

The kindness daily planner and karma journal is based on the idea that it's much easier to get things done when you have a simple prompt. This tool helps you plan, journal and track your kindness using things we've covered in *Karma in Action*.

5 Days of Karmic Kindness

Begin today! Imagine what it can be like. And remember, laugh a little and appreciate if some old bad stuff gets cleared out. It only gets better!

We've given you 5 days so you can get started planting seeds and enjoy the process of putting karma into action!

Hugs,
Joanne & Booth

My project is . . .

_____

my four karmic partners are . . . (the branches of my tree)

_____

_____

_____

_____

I'd like to get this done by . . .

_____

Exactly how will it look if I am really successful at this task?

Note: *Specifics! Let my imagination fill this page in. Color if I like, little sketches too. It's all good.*

SEED THE CHANGE
YOU WISH TO BE

—Booth Aster

In full appreciation of Mahatma Gandhi

5 DAYS OF KARMA AND KINDNESS FOR THE BIGGER YOU

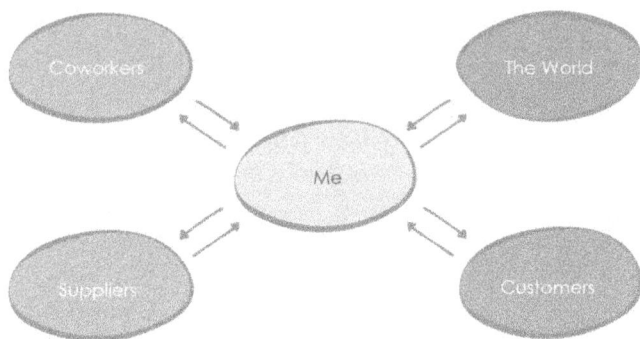

Imagine what 5 days of kindness feels like:

Write or Draw

Cross out each day as you go

| 1 | 2 | 3 | 4 | 5 |

I will celebrate doing these 5 days by:

Write or Draw

DAY & DATE: _____

GET STARTED WELL: Morning: Meditation ❑ Yoga ❑

Plan Your Beneficial Actions for Today

Karmic Partner	Who	What	Done
Coworker			
Customer			
Supplier			
World			

Creative space to riff, draw, and write notes:

DURING THE DAY: Do your beneficial actions! (tick them off as you go)

Skillful noticing: Eating

Are you putting good fuel or poor quality fuel into your system?

Fuel	Sugars	Carbs	Fats	Stimulants	Other
Meal					
Snack					
Meal					
Snack					
Meal					
Snack					

Skillful noticing of your mind in action (circle or check where appropriate)

Your words: *Your actions:*

kind words / idle chatter   thoughtful / disruptive

You took a break every 30 minutes ❑

BEFORE YOU GO TO BED: Skillfully notice

1. **Your intentions:** Beneficial actions done as planned? Yes/No

2. **Your mind:** (minutes on)

On the computer / devices: _____	News: reading or listen to: _____	Unnecessary time on the phone: _____

3. **Yourself in action:**

Ethics in action: Personal act of kindness:

_____   _____

_____   _____

_____   _____

_____   _____

_____

Now fall asleep thinking of the good things you've done today!

DAY & DATE: _____

Plan Your Beneficial Actions for Today

Karmic Partner	Who	What	Done
Coworker			
Customer			
Supplier			
World			

Creative space to riff, draw, and write notes:

DURING THE DAY: Do your beneficial actions! (tick them off as you go)

Skillful noticing: Eating

Are you putting good fuel or poor quality fuel into your system?

Fuel	Sugars	Carbs	Fats	Stimulants	Other
Meal					
Snack					
Meal					
Snack					
Meal					
Snack					

Skillful noticing of your mind in action (circle or check where appropriate)

Your words:	*Your actions:*
kind words / idle chatter	thoughtful / disruptive

You took a break every 30 minutes ❑

BEFORE YOU GO TO BED: Skilfully notice

1. **Your intentions:** Beneficial actions done as planned? Yes/No

2. **Your mind:** (minutes on)

   On the computer / devices: _____   News: reading or listen to: _____   Unnecessary time on the phone: _____

3. **Yourself in action:**

   Ethics in action: Personal act of kindness:

   _____   _____
   _____   _____
   _____   _____
   _____   _____
   _____   _____

Now fall asleep thinking of the good things you've done today!

DAY & DATE: _____

GET STARTED WELL: Morning: Meditation ❑ Yoga ❑

Plan Your Beneficial Actions for Today

Karmic Partner	Who	What	Done
Coworker			
Customer			
Supplier			
World			

Creative space to riff, draw, and write notes:

DURING THE DAY: Do your beneficial actions! (tick them off as you go)

Skillful noticing: Eating

Are you putting good fuel or poor quality fuel into your system?

Fuel	Sugars	Carbs	Fats	Stimulants	Other
Meal					
Snack					
Meal					
Snack					
Meal					
Snack					

Skillful noticing of your mind in action (circle or check where appropriate)

Your words:	*Your actions:*
kind words / idle chatter	thoughtful / disruptive

You took a break every 30 minutes ❑

BEFORE YOU GO TO BED: Skillfully notice

1. **Your intentions:** Beneficial actions done as planned? Yes/No

2. **Your mind:** (minutes on)

   On the computer / devices: _____   News: reading or listen to: _____   Unnecessary time on the phone: _____

3. **Yourself in action:**

Ethics in action:	Personal act of kindness:
_____	_____
_____	_____
_____	_____
_____	_____
_____	_____

Now fall asleep thinking of the good things you've done today!

DAY & DATE: _____

Plan Your Beneficial Actions for Today

Karmic Partner	Who	What	Done
Coworker			
Customer			
Supplier			
World			

Creative space to riff, draw, and write notes:

DURING THE DAY: Do your beneficial actions! (tick them off as you go)

Skillful noticing: Eating

Are you putting good fuel or poor quality fuel into your system?

Fuel	Sugars	Carbs	Fats	Stimulants	Other
Meal					
Snack					
Meal					
Snack					
Meal					
Snack					

Skillful noticing of your mind in action (circle or check where appropriate)

Your words:	Your actions:
kind words / idle chatter	thoughtful / disruptive

You took a break every 30 minutes ❑

BEFORE YOU GO TO BED: Skillfully notice

1. Your intentions: Beneficial actions done as planned? Yes/No

2. Your mind: (minutes on)

On the computer / devices: _____   News: reading or listen to: _____   Unnecessary time on the phone: _____

3. Yourself in action:

Ethics in action: Personal act of kindness:

_____   _____

_____   _____

_____   _____

_____   _____

_____   _____

Now fall asleep thinking of the good things you've done today!

DAY & DATE: _____

Plan Your Beneficial Actions for Today

Karmic Partner	Who	What	Done
Coworker			
Customer			
Supplier			
World			

Creative space to riff, draw, and write notes:

DURING THE DAY: Do your beneficial actions! (tick them off as you go)

Skillful noticing: Eating

Are you putting good fuel or poor quality fuel into your system?

Fuel	Sugars	Carbs	Fats	Stimulants	Other
Meal					
Snack					
Meal					
Snack					
Meal					
Snack					

Skillful noticing of your mind in action (circle or check where appropriate)

Your words:	*Your actions:*
kind words / idle chatter	thoughtful / disruptive

You took a break every 30 minutes ❑

BEFORE YOU GO TO BED: Skillfully notice

1. **Your intentions:** Beneficial actions done as planned? Yes/No

2. **Your mind:** (minutes on)

On the computer / devices: _____   News: reading or listen to: _____   Unnecessary time on the phone: _____

3. **Yourself in action:**

Ethics in action: Personal act of kindness:

_____   _____

_____   _____

_____   _____

_____   _____

_____   _____

Now fall asleep thinking of the good things you've done today!

Skillful Noticing

How do you feel? What's happening?

And celebrate!!!

Lots of space for you to write, draw, and color the good
things you see happening in your life.

**ALL WORK IS EMPTY SAVE
WHERE THERE IS LOVE**

—Khalil Gibran

Celebrate!!

And reflect again on all the good things you've done
for others over the course of this project.

There is no expiration on remembering and
appreciating good things.

Give It Forward

Three ideas to add even more karma to your life:

Pick a new project.

Share the secret to your success with others.
(Teaching is very powerful karma.)

Plant more seeds to help the world be better.
(Remember the B1G1 model.)

https://b1g1.com/connect/KIA.

May your life be magic, may your love and friendships be deep, and may all your projects add to the kindness, life, and beauty of the earth and our souls.

Thank you for putting Karma in Action,

Joanne, Booth, and Anna

The Science Behind the Ideas

At first, I took karma and kindness simply as an applied approach to the Golden Rule. Through study, I realized these ideas are backed by solid neuroscience. Here are some of the highlights.

Our brain has two major categories of response:

FIRE—responses involving fear, fight, and flight.

DESIRE—responses involving interest, curiosity, and attraction.

Many of our default behaviors are fear based. We even use fear to create action. What fear does neurologically is to trigger our action station, or hijack the amygdala. The downside is that our thinking is poor when emotions are so high, it's tough on our adrenal glands, and it can lead to burnout.

When you peel back karma and kindness, the daily actions involved are about keeping you calm and healthy. Adrenals are happy. The amygdala learns to relax. Stress decreases. Attention span increases. Relationships get better with a constructive mental state and full command of your attention.

Yoga and meditation influence various parts of the brain:

* Frontal lobe—this plans and reasons. It's the noisy part of our brain and it switches off during yoga and meditation, helping you detach and relax.
* Thalamus—this sends motor and sensory signals to the cerebral cortex. Slowing it down in yoga and meditation helps you keep calm.
* Parietal lobe—gives us our sense of time. In yoga and meditation, it slows down so you experience more time, slower time. This lowers your stress and anxiety levels.
* Reticular activating system—this keeps your brain alert, looks for patterns, and helps you respond. During yoga and meditation, reticular activity slows down, allowing you to keep calm and peaceful. This also allows you to see new patterns.

For those familiar with positive psychology, you'll find karma and kindness are a practical disciplined yet relaxed approach to putting the insights of this field into practice.

About the Author

I'm writing this to you in the first person. After all, we've been on a journey together and have got to know each other a bit.

I ran my first $10 million business at 24, before going on to lead the Financial Services Consulting Practice for PricewatehouseCoopers in Thailand. It was while living in Thailand that I saw these practices in daily action. I moved to Singapore and became a member of the IT Executive Committee for an international bank. There I learned that when we had faith in people and focused on the good, when we were kind and respectful, the big disruptive billion-dollar digital projects went amazingly well.

Over my years in the corporate world, I burnt out three times. I realized I needed to find another way. I went to the University of Oxford and HÈC Paris to research and reflect. During this time I developed the 8-Fold Path to Success, a methodology for business growth, otherwise known, as I began to have more fun with my clients, as Unicorning™!

When my wonderful friend Lynna introduced me to Geshe Michael Roach, to the Diamond Wisdom team, and to the teaching of the Dalai Lama, I felt that I'd found the broader structure in which everything made sense. Most importantly, this structure helped me create a format that works for me in daily life—both as human being and as a business founder.

I use it to stretch my wings as an artist, a long-held dream of mine. Using these principles my artist identity, Booth Aster, has illustrated books that are in museums and has created a body of work that has been exhibited in museums and is included in collections on four continents.

I hope Karma In Action brings you as much joy and success as it has me.

Do reach out to me on LinkedIn or email me at:

Joanne@KarmaInAction.works

There may be a karmic gift awaiting you!

Joanne & Booth

www.ingramcontent.com/pod-product-compliance
Lightning Source LLC
LaVergne TN
LVHW011212080426
835508LV00007B/744